D1448849

# Words of Wisdom and Magic
from the *Kalevala*

*"Come and listen now,*
*if you've never heard before,*
*the joy of everlasting song,*
*the cadence of the kantele."*

41: 13-161

J. Koskela: *"Runonlaulajat"*
"Rune Singers" wood carving

# Words

## of

# WISDOM

## and

# MAGIC

## from the

# *Kalevala*

"Wise words never die,
Although the mighty pass away."

17: 523-526

*Translated and compiled by Richard Impola*

*Illustrations by Diane Heusinkveld*

Penfield
Press

*"It's great to be an invited guest
but better yet to crash the gate."*

27: 199-200

Translations are from the 1944 edition of the *Kalevala*, published by the *Kalevan Ritarit Ylin Maja*, Hancock, Michigan.

Edited by Joan Liffring-Zug Bourret and Dorothy Crum
Associate Editors: Melinda Bradnan, Dwayne Bourret
and Walter Meyer

Books by mail:
Add $4 shipping cost to price listed for one book;
    additional books .50 each.
1998 prices subject to change.

*Words of Wisdom and Magic from the* Kalevala $12.95
(this book)
*Suomi Specialties: Finnish Celebrations, Recipes and Traditions*
    by Sinikka Grönberg Garcia $12.95
*Finnish Proverbs* translated by Inkeri Väänänen-Jensen $10.95
*FinnFun* by Bernhard Hillila $12.95
*Fantastically Finnish: Recipes and Traditions* $7.95

Penfield Press — 215 Brown Street — Iowa City, Iowa 52245

ISBN 1-57216-041-1
Library of Congress 98-65714                    © 1998 Richard Impola

# The Translator

On retirement from college teaching in 1983, Richard Impola embarked on a new career as a translator of Finnish literature. He holds the Ph.D. in English Literature from Columbia University and has taught at the Michigan Technological University and at the SUNY (State University of New York) College at New Paltz.

Born in 1923, his boyhood home was in Upper Michigan, the point of entry for so many immigrants from Finland. His maternal grandparents (from Pudasjärvi) arrived in Michigan in 1880-81. Cousins tell a story of his grandfather's carving out the rotted core of a huge fallen log for a hut to live in during that first winter while he hauled firewood to the copper smelter at the Delaware Mine in Michigan's Copper Country to earn money for his family's passage.

His paternal grandparents were reindeer dealers in northeastern Finland before buying up a tract of land near Siikajoki, on the west coast, where they settled in 1886. His father, Jacob, left there for America in 1893.

During his college years in New York, Richard and his wife, Helvi (nee Thors, also of Finnish descent), from New York City, were active in the cultural life of the Finnish community which still existed in that city. They took part in stage plays, and he sang with the city's Finnish male choir. Both are hopelessly addicted to Finnish folk music and dance. Their son Paul is in the Civil Service in Albany, New York; son Tom teaches English in Japan, and daughter Karen is the folk music person at KUNI, the University of Northern Iowa's public broadcasting station.

Brushing up on the language for a trip to Finland, he

became fascinated by the literature of that country. Reino Hannula, the publisher of *Finn Heritage*, suggested that he translate a novel by Finland's most popular author, Kalle Päätalo. Since then, he has translated or edited at least a half-dozen books. Two of his translated novels, *Seven Brothers* and *Storm Over the Land*, have been adopted for use in a number of college and university classes. Another, *Hand in Hand*, has been re-translated from the English into Norwegian and Danish.

His translations of poetry and short stories have appeared in such publications as *Twentieth Century Scandinavian Poetry*, *Nordic Women Writers* (forthcoming), *New Finnish Fiction*, *Sycamore Review*, the *Journal of Anglo-Scandinavian Poetry*, and *Dimension — Contemporary Nordic Literature*. He has spoken on Finnish literature at a number of gatherings, and in 1993 he was awarded the American-Scandinavian Foundation's Inger Sjöberg Prize for translation.

*Helsingin Sanomat (Helsinki News)*, Finland's equivalent to the *New York Times*, has described him as the most effective proponent of Finnish literature in North America.

# Contents

# Introduction

*The Kalevala played an important part in developing a sense of identity among Finns, and in the eventual emergence of Finland as a nation.*

This selection from the poetry of Finland's national epic, the *Kalevala*, can only suggest the richness of the work. The work itself is a compilation from the oral poetry of the Finns, written down and shaped into an epic poem by Dr. Elias Lönnrot. Its subject matter accumulated over many centuries, and includes everything from tales of mythical figures with superhuman powers to touchingly human stories. It opens with a story of creation and closes with a version of the birth of Jesus.

On February 28, 1835, Elias Lönnrot signed his name to the Foreward of the *Kalevala* or *Old Poems of Karelia from the Ancient Times of the Finnish People*. The day has become a national day for the celebration of Finnish culture. However, it is Lönnrot's expanded and rearranged version of 1849 that almost everyone knows as the *Kalevala*. In 1999, the 150th anniversary of this publication will be marked by an international congress on epic poetry at the University of Turku. The *Kalevala* is of particular interest to scholars because it survived as oral poetry hundreds of years longer than other epics.

The stories in the *Kalevala* are grouped mainly about three figures: Väinämöinen, great word-magician; Lemminkäinen, the Don Juan of Finnish legend, and the great smith Ilmarinen, forger of the dome of the sky and of the magical mill, the Sampo. Other figures include Louhi, the mistress of the North, and her daughter, the bride of Ilmarinen. Further characters from the work are the young Aino, promised in marriage to the aged Väinämöinen, and the tragic Kullervo. Many of the figures from the *Kalevala* have become familiar to the world in the work of poets, musicians, and painters. The poem has been translated into forty-four languages.

We hope that the sampling in this book will lead people to read more of the *Kalevala*. A selection as brief as this cannot claim to represent the entire work. The excerpts here have been chosen for their intrinsic value. In most cases it is the power of expression which has led to their inclusion, in others the cultural content or the folk wisdom they embody. Frequently it is the eloquent expression of a general human emotion which has determined the choice.

A characteristic of much Finnish literature is its emphasis on capturing in words the very feel of life itself. Most epics deal with war and heroic deeds. The *Kalevala* does include such adventures, but the poem is unique among epics in the range of subject matter it embraces. Despite the exoticism of its setting and the shamanist mysticism of some of its content, a reader often has the feeling of being closely in touch with a life we can all relate to. In her book, *Philosophy in a New Key*, Susan Langer writes of Aino:

"...in the *Kalevala*, there are sudden passages of human import set in its strange, mystical frame.....her [Aino's] plight is realistic and touching....Here is the beginning of the higher mythology, wherein the world is essentially the stage for human life, the setting of the true epic, which is human and social."

The wedding episodes — the hazing of the bride, the advice to bride and groom, the comments on in-law relationships — bring us close to the life of the times. And although the central figure, Väinämöinen, is possessed of superhuman powers, he behaves very much like a foolish old man in his efforts to court young women. Lemminkäinen, too, is a great magician, yet he is a womanizer, and he is rash and boastful at times.

The passages translated usually fall into the four-beat meter of the *Kalevala* line, although I have occasionally used a three-beat line to avoid padding the English. English tends to be naturally iambic, as opposed to the trochaic patterns of Finnish. I have made no effort to follow the trochaic pattern if the result would have been to distort the natural flow of the English language. At times I have skipped lines within a passage. In such cases the line numbers indicate the first and last lines of a passage from which the quoted lines have been taken. My goal has been to produce an enjoyable and readable text, which, I hope, is still true to the spirit of the original.

The fact that the *Kalevala,* a poem, was really instrumental in the Finns' developing a sense of identity certainly has something to do with the prestige of poetry — and literature in general among Finns. Many Finnish writers have written both prose and poetry — there aren't, for example, many American novelists that do that. There is a group in Finland that holds an annual competition with poetry on modern subjects written in the *Kalevala* meter.

Then there is the language — with its many vowels it can, like the Italian, be very musical. It is filled with images, particularly from nature, which Finns tend to be fond of. The American poet, Henry Wadsworth Longfellow, who was interested in metrical experiments, used the *Kalevala* meter for his *Hiawatha.* Quite a feat, since the nature of the two languages is so different. English falls naturally into an iambic beat, an unaccented followed by an accented syllable — for example: a book, I think, hello, to speak, etc. — while in Finnish every word is accented on the first syllable and the natural pattern is trochaic — ko-ti, kau-nis, kul-ku-ri. The fact that Finnish has no articles (a, the) only serves to emphasize the trochaic pattern of the language. Each line of the *Kalevala* meter is made up of four trochees (trochaic tetrameter). Longfellow became acquainted with the meter in a German translation of the *Kalevala*.

A guide to the reading of the *Kalevala*, based on Elias Lönnrot's prefatory summaries to each runo, is appended to this book. It is intended to give the reader a frame of reference for following the action of the epic.

For the Finnish text of the *Kalevala*, I have used the edition published by the *Kalevan Ritarit Ylin Maja* in Hancock, Michigan, 1944.

— Richard Impola, Ph.D.

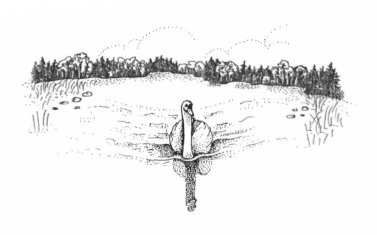

# The spell of the oral tradition

Brother dear, my best of friends,
comrade of my childhood years!
Come and clasp your hands in mine,
let our fingers intertwine.
Let us chant the cherished words,
those best songs that cast a spell,
on those who love to listen,
the young folk of the nation,
the rising generation:
These my father sang to me,
whittling the handle of an ax;
these my mother taught to me
as she spun her distaff...
I a scamp with beard of milk
tumbling about before her knees...

1: 11-43

Veli kulta, veikkoseni,
kaunis kasvinkumppalini!
Lyökämme käsi kätehen,
sormet sormien lomahan,
lauloaksemme hyviä,
parahia pannaksemme,
kuulla noien kultaisien
tietä mielitehtoisien
nuorisossa nousevassa,

kansassa kasuavassa:
Niit' ennen isoni lauloi
kirvesvartta vuollessansa;
niitä äitini opetti
väätessänsä värttinätä,
minun...
eessä polven pyöriessä
maitopartana pahaisna...

1: 11-43

# Nature
### and
## Poetry

Other songs and spells I learned,
snatched from the wayside, plucked from heather,
torn from thickets, stripped from saplings,
rubbed from haytips, gleaned from hedges
as I drove the cows to pasture,
over golden honeyed hills
tending brindled Bess and Blackie...

the frost spoke verse,
the rain pattered poems,
the wind blew words,
the sea waves sang,
the birds wove rhymes
and treetops told me tales.

1: 51-70

# Solitude

I've heard it said, I've read in verse:
we are alone when night comes on,
alone when the morning dawns.

1: 103-106

## Arrogant youth

A father's wisdom is fine,
a mother's even better.
But my own is best of all.

3: 52-54

## Healing

Water is the oldest balm,
foam of rapids first elixir,
the Creator first to drive out ills,
God the primal healer.

3: 199-202

## Content with little

I don't want imported woolens,
fine wheat bread so thinly sliced.
I can live on very little,
be content with coarser clothing,
I can thrive on crusts of rye,
here at home with my good father,
my loving mother by my side.

4: 25-30

15

# Diet for a
# Beauty

Eat pure butter for a year,
you'll grow more buxom than the rest.
Next year eat your fill of pork,
'twill make you the liveliest by far.
The third year feast yourself on creamcakes,
you'll be the fairest of them all.

4: 121-126

# Adornment

Bind your brow with band of silk.
Deck your forehead all in gold.
Hang bright beads about your neck
and golden crosses on your breast.

4: 167-170

*Sio nyt silkit silmillesi,*
*kullat kulmille kohota,*
*kaulahan heleät helmet,*
*kullanristit rinnoillesi!*

4: 167-170

# Bliss

What is it like to be happy?
What is the feeling of bliss?
The thoughts of a joyful person
are like the rippling of water.
A happy person's mind
is like the waves on a pond.

4: 197-202

# Aino's Grief

Better had it been for me
better had I ne'er been born.
Never seen the light of day
in this wretched age.
Never grown to maidenhood
in these woeful times.

4: 217-222

# A *daughter's* lament

This is why I weep, poor girl,
weep away my days and nights.
You gave me, your poor girl, away,
promised me, your own child,
to be an old man's property,
to pleasure him in his latter years,
to take care of a dodderer.

4: 235-242

# A *mother's* remorse

Alas, you mothers, don't you ever
never ever in your lives,
try to wheedle your daughters,
to sweet-talk your own children
into wedding against their will
as I, poor mother, did.

4: 439-444

## The ideal wife

I would have been the one
to cuddle underneath your arm,
to be forever by your side,
to make your bed,
fluff up your pillow,
clean your little house,
sweep your floors,
kindle your fires
and tend them through the day,
bake thick loaves of honey bread,
bring you your stoup of beer
and set out your meals.

5: 110-122

## Homesickness

I will forever weep
for having left my own land,
my own familiar stamping grounds,
to stop at unknown doors,
to stand before the gates of strangers.
Every tree here stings me,
every branch slaps at me,
birch trees thump and alders slash me:
the wind alone is known to me,
only the sun I see is the same.

7: 253-264

## No place like home

Better to drink at home
water from a birch-bark shoe,
than honey from a golden goblet
sipped at the table of strangers.

7: 285-288

## Single or wedded bliss?

Bright is a sunny day,
brighter still a free maid's life.
Cold is iron in a frost,
colder the lot of a daughter-in-law.
A girl in her father's house
is like a berry in rich earth,
but at her father-in-law's
she's like a dog in chains.

8: 71-78

## A higher power

Greater floods have been contained,
mightier inundations checked,
by just three words of the Creator
who holds sway over causes deep.

8: 275-278

# Prudence

You who are the future,
members of the rising generation,
do not act out of defiance,
build a boat because you're challenged.
It is God who sets the course,
the Creator who decides the end.
That is beyond the strength of man,
even of the mightiest.

9: 579-586

# Male ego

Let women doubt what they can do,
those weaklings leave a job undone.
Even the worst of men keeps trying,
even the feeblest male works on!

10: 291-294

# Lemminkäinen's revenge

I made a mockery of the maids,
revenged me on the sainted ones
for making me the butt of jokes,
laughing at me for so long.
I carried off the best of them,
laid her on my sled robes....

11: 353-358

# A good daughter-in-law

Thanks be to God alone,
praise be to the Creator
for a good daughter-in-law:
good at blowing up the fire,
the very best at spinning,
skilled at weaving cloth,
strong to wield the laundry paddle,
wash the clothes as white as snow.

11: 373-380

# Spirit of adventure

I don't care to stay at home!
Sweeter is water from a stream,
lapped from a tarry rudder oar
than any beer that's brewed at home.
I value money won in war
more than all your home-got gold
turned up by the blade of plow.

12: 74-104

# On infidelity

It's dreadful for one lone man
to have two women in his bed.

12: 121-122

# Brevity

A song is good when it ends betimes,
a verse is beautiful when it's brief;
a song that's neatly capped,
sticks much better in the mind.

12: 409-412

# Money is for spending

… … …money… … … …
wears out in wallets,
coins lose their luster in a chest,
when nobody trades for gold
or strikes up a deal for silver.

14: 223-230

# Mother love

Long she hunted for her lost one,
long she searched but did not find him,
even asked the trees about him,
longing for her lost one.

15: 127-130

## Humility

By myself I can do nothing,
all alone I helpless am,
unless God grant me His mercy,
unless the true Creator act.

15: 637-640

## Wait your turn

What a fool you are, my man,
what a dimwit dunderhead!
To come to Manala for no reason,
undiseased to Tuonela.
Better if you stayed away,
went in safety to your land.
Countless thousands enter here,
Few there are who e'er return.

16: 265-272

## Divine aid

God will not reject the good
or let the virtuous be lost.

17: 183-184

# The power of words

Wise words will never die
although the mighty pass away.

## Sauna

*Siitä seppo Ilmarinen*
*kävi itse kylpemähän*
*sekä kylpi kylläksensä,*
*valelihe valkeaksi;*
*pesi silmät sirkeäksi,*
*silmäkulmat kukkeaksi,*
*kaulansa kananmuniksi,*
*koko varren valkeaksi.*

18: 321-328

Then the smith, that Ilmarinen
went to take his sauna bath,
bathed unto his heart's content,
splashed until his skin was white,
till his eyes were sparkling bright,
his brow was of the lily's sheen,
his neck the hue of fresh-peeled eggs,
and all his body clean.

18: 321-328

## Misogyny

Women are forever busy.
There's always work they have to do—
basking in the chimney corner,
lolling lazy in their beds.

18: 512-515

## Why marry?

I don't want a man for wealth—
won't have him for his mind.
It's a fetching face that gets me,
and a handsome build to match.

18: 639-642

## Jack will have his Jill

… … … … …
for 'tis hard to hide a maiden,
keep a long-haired girl secure.
Though you build a stony castle
far out on the open sea,
keep your maidens in seclusion,
rear your chicks in solitude,
there's no way they'll stay concealed,
grow up there in isolation,
men of note will come to court them,
suitors great from all the land…

19: 487-496

# Old Väinämöinen's
# *lament*

*Voi minua, mies kuluista,*
*kun en tuota tuntenunna,*
*naia nuorella iällä,*
*etsiä elon ajalla!*

*Kaikkiansa se katuvi,*
*joka nuorta naimistansa,*
*lasna lapsen saamistansa,*
*pienenä perehtimistä.*

19: 503-510

Woe is me — old, worn-out wretch,
I should have known this earlier,
married at a tender age,
found my treasure in good time.
He would rue all things,
who regrets being wed while young,
and having children early,
while in his budding years.

19: 503-510

# Guests *arriving?*

Wait while I look the place over,
see to things around the house.
Have the tables been well washed?
The benches rinsed with water?
The smooth floors swept all clean?
Boards brushed free of litter?

21: 147-152

## The *wedding feast*

There was salmon on the trays
with a good side dish of pork,
cups were filled to overflowing,
dishes spilling o'er the sides,
all for invited guests to feast on,
but especially for the groom.

21: 233-238

# One man's opinion

*Olipa ukko uunin päällä.*
*Tuopa tuon sanoiksi virkki:*
*"Ei ole lasten laululoista,*
*kurjien kujerteloista:*
*valehia lasten laulut,*
*tyhjiä tytärten virret!*
*Anna virsi viisahalle…"*

21: 307-313

There was an old man atop the oven.
He spoke his mind in these words:
"Put no stock in children's verses,
croonings of these juveniles:
children's songs are only lies,
girlies' chantings empty nothings.
Let the wise men do the singing…"

21: 307-313

## Reason to wed?

… … … … …
as I grew up, I kept repeating:
"You, my girl are not a woman
while still living off your parents…
Only then you'll be a woman
when you're in your husband's house."

22: 132-137

# I told you so

Remember all the times I told you—
repeated it a hundred times:
"Don't let a sweetheart charm you,
lure you with his smiling lips.
Put no faith in loving looks
or feast your eyes on splendid legs."

22: 189-194

I told you so,
gave you good warning,
repeated it over and over again:
"Don't go to Pohjola!"

28: 167-170

# In-laws

In her father's house
a girl is like a king...
but in her husband's home
she's like a Russian slave...

22: 314-319

*Niin neito ison kotona,*
*kuin kuningas linnassansa...*
*niin miniä miehelässä,*
*kuin vanki Venäehellä...*

22: 314-319

# Advice to a bride

When you leave this house
take all other things with you,
but leave behind your chest of dreams
for the girls at home to have.
Toss your songs on a seat,
or lay them on the ledge of a window,
leave girlishness to the sauna switch,
and giddiness to scraps of selvage,
abandon bad traits to the oven-shelf,
leave laziness on the floor!
Or offer it to the bridesmaid
to toss away in a thicket...

23: 35-54

# More advice to the bride

... ... ... ... ... ...
men can be a burden,
even the very best of them.
Strictness will be needed
if a husband's house is slipshod.
A wife must be dependable
if her husband is a bungler.

23: 85-90

31

# A *woman's work*

Don't dawdle around the barn,
loiter around the lamb pen.
When you've cleaned up there,
and seen to all the stock,
waste no further time,
but rush back to the house.
There a child is crying,
wrapped up in its blankets....

Keep track of all your spoons,
know the number of your dishes,
see that dogs don't nick them,
cats don't carry them away...

23: 341-344

# The rowan (mountain ash)

*Pyhät on pihlajat pihalla,*
*pyhät oksat pihlajissa,*
*pyhät lehvät oksasilla,*
*marjaset sitäi pyhemmät,*
*joilla neittä neuvotahan*
*nuoren miehen mieltä myöten,*
*sulhosen syäntä myöten.*

23: 223-230

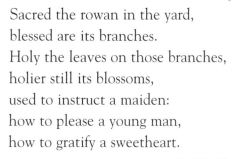

Sacred the rowan in the yard,
blessed are its branches.
Holy the leaves on those branches,
holier still its blossoms,
used to instruct a maiden:
how to please a young man,
how to gratify a sweetheart.

23: 223-230

## Appetites

Its mouth lured the fox to a snare,
its taste buds trapped a weasel.
Desire draws a maid to a man,
her nature leads her to his home.

23: 519-522

# Advice to the groom

When you visit with your lady,
never leave her sitting silent,
moping around in corners!

24: 105-108

... ... ... ... ... ...

don't bar your cellar door to her, nor
forbid her to enter the storehouse!

24: 151-152

Never, my poor lover,
never teach her with a whip,
nor abuse her like a slave...

24: 187-189

# Parting

... ... ... ... ...

my time to leave draws nearer,
the farewell hour is at hand,
misery for me to go,
sorrowful this parting hour,
sad to leave this splendid home,
lovely farmyard of my youth...

24: 303-308

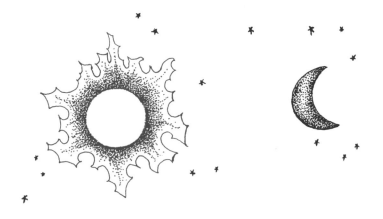

# *Consolation*

The sun of the Creator shines,
the moon too glows,
stars sparkle overhead,
the Great Bear stretches out
across the sky in other zones
in other places in this world
not just in my father's yard…

24: 355-361

# Leaving home

Farewell to all of these:
Fields and berried forests,
flowery lanes and heather heaths,
island-dotted lakes
deep whitefish waters
fir-covered hills
and dales bedecked with birches.

24: 455-462

*Jätän kaikki terveheksi:*
*maat ja metsät marjoinensa,*
*kujavieret kukkinensa,*
*kankahat kanervinensa,*
*järvet saoin saarinensa,*
*syvät salmet siikoinensa,*
*hyvät kummut kuusinensa,*
*korpinotkot koivuinensa.*

24: 455-462

Farewell, lakes and shores,
fields and firs upon the hill,
tall pine trees,
the chokecherry behind the house,
the juniper on the well-path,
stalks of berries, stands of hay,
clumps of willows, roots of spruce,
leaves of alder, bark of birch!

24: 467-476

Jää hyvästi, järven rannat,
järven rannat, pellon penkat,
kaikki mäntyset mäellä,
puut pitkät petäjikössä,
tuomikko tuvan takana,
katajikko kaivotiellä,
marjan varret, heinän korret,
pajupehkot, kuusen juuret,
lepän lehvät, koivun kuoret!

24: 467-476

# Creativity

Singing is the task of poets,
as calling is for springtime cuckoos,
as weaving for the weaver spirit.
Even Lapland children sing...

25: 425-429

# A man's work

First they praised the master
who turned a swamp into a haven,
made the wilderness a home:
felled the sturdy trunks of pine trees,
stacked them at a landing,
built with them on solid ground
a fine home for his family...

25: 471-480

# Mother of the bride

Often the good housewife,
keen caretaker of the home,
was heard to rise before the cockcrow,
getting ready for the wedding,
preparing all the foods,
baking all the breads,
brewing up the beer.

25: 535-542

# Word magic

Then old Väinämöinen
grew a blue forest with song,
in it a smooth-barked oak,
along with the rowan he needed;
from them he sang up a basket sleigh,
fitted with runners and struts,
a collar bow for the horse,
bent into shape with his song...

25: 717-724

# Machismo

Women see death everywhere,
threats of doom on every side.
All this a man takes lightly,
shows not a hint of concern...

26: 107-110

# Evil

Only evil comes from evil,
the wicked vomit wickedness...

26: 717-718

She was the blind spawn of Tuoni,
the old ogress, Loviatar,
the worst of Tuoni's daughters,
nastiest caster of spells,
the root of all evil,
source of a thousand disasters.
Her hue was shaded toward black,
her skin the color of nausea.

45: 23-30

# Etiquette?

It's great to be an invited guest,
but better yet to crash the gate.

27: 199-200

# Song

*Vielä lauloi Lemminkäinen,*
*vielä lauloi ja saneli,*
*lauloi hiekat helmilöiksi,*
*kivet kaikki kiiltäviksi,*
*puut kaikki punertaviksi,*
*kukat kullankarvaisiksi.*

29: 165-170

Lemminkäinen still kept singing,
pouring out his store of words:
Sang the seas to pearly beads,
sang a sheen on all the stones,
sang a ruddy tint on trees,
sang the flowers to glowing gold.

29: 165-170

## Playboy

Free and easy Lemminkäinen
made his way around the place,
romping with the village girls,
dallying with the long-haired beauties.
Whichever way he turned his head,
a kiss was blown in his direction.
Wherever he reached out a hand,
another hand was there to clasp it.

29: 223-230

# Longing

The girls who dwelt on the cape
sat on the blue seashore,
gazing this way and that
across the blue sea waters.
One waited for her brother,
another for her dad;
she who waited most eagerly
was waiting for her lover.

29: 49-56

## A sad note

The time has come for me to part,
to leave this place, be on my way.
No more to frolic with the girls,
no more romping with my pretties.

29: 347-350

# Why?

Lemminkäinen is leaving—
because he misses his own home—
longs to see those fields of his,
strawberries growing on his land,
raspberries ripening on his hill,
he longs for the maidens on his cape,
the chicks that shelter in his yard.

29: 369-376

# Fending off the cold

Chill the swamps and chill the soil,
chill the cold rocks colder still.
Freeze the willow by the water,
crack the galls on aspen trees,
peel the bark from birches,
nip the spruce if need be,
but never touch a person's skin,
a hair of any mother's son!

30: 195-202

# A mother's lament

Woe is me, my son is gone,
My sole support, alas, is gone,
gone to sow the crops of Tuoni,
harrow the fields of Manala.
Woe is me, here are his bows,
they hang neglected on the wall,
drying out in idleness.
Birds grow fat out in the woods,
partridge preen themselves in copses,
bears ramp and rage about,
deer prance out in the fields.

30: 405-416

# Appearances

Many a loaf looks good on top,
the crust may be all sleek and smooth,
but inside it there is straw,
husks and chaff beneath the shell.

33: 77-80

# Kullervo's *despair*

Dear God, never create a child to wander
under the sky alone like me,
without a father or a mother,
like a gull 'mongst rocky crags.
Day will dawn for the swallow,
the sun will rise for the sparrow,
there is joy for the birds of the air,
but never any joy for me.
No sun will ever shine on me,
never, ever in my lifetime.

34: 55-70

············ ··· ··· ···

Better off I were
never to have been born,
never to have seen the light of day,
or been thrust into this world.

35: 279-282

# Who lives by the sword

He who fights without a cause,
purposely seeks out a war,
he is sure to die in battle:
a sword will cut him down,
a saber end his days.

36: 11-16

# A mother's grief

You cannot know a mother's mind,
see into a mother's heart.
I will weep for you
when I hear that you are dead,
gone from among us,
lost to your kin.
I will flood the house with tears,
weep waves upon the floor,
weep awash the barnyard,
weep the snow to glare ice,
melt the ice to thawed ground,
weep the ground to greenery,
and wither the green with weeping.

36: 135-145

# On raising children

Do not, people of the future,
ever raise a child askew,
let a stupid nursemaid rock him,
a stranger lull him to sleep.
A child who is wrongly reared,
one who is stupidly hushed,
never will be wise…

36: 351-357

# On gold and silver

Then Väinämöinen forbade
the suitor from still waters,
forbade the growing nation,
the rising generation,
to bow down to gold
to be swayed by silver.

37: 233-238

# Sailing

It's joy for a boat to sail,
to ride bobbing over the waves
as the broad waters gleam;
to skim across the open sea
as the wind rocks the boat,
and a wave drives it on—
the west wind whips up waves,
the south wind drives the ship.

39: 45-52

# Forethought

Precaution never sinks a ship,
nor does a prop spill a haystack.

39: 416-417

# The kantele

Come and listen now,
if you've never heard before,
the joy of everlasting song,
the cadence of the kantele.

     ... ... ... ... ... ...

Väinämöinen played on...
Not a single four-foot creature
that skipped or trotted in the woods
could refrain from listening,
from wondering at the joyous sound.
Squirrels came scampering along the boughs,
weasels settled on the fence,
moose cavorted on the heath,
even lynxes celebrated.

In the swamp the wolf awoke
from his den in a grove of spruce.
The bear roused from his lair
among the pines on a heath.

Tapio, sharp old forest spirit,
with all his people, men and maids,
climbed to the crest of a hill
to listen to the strumming.

All the birds of the air
came flocking on the wing
to listen with awe and delight.

The eagle soared on high,
the hawk cut through the clouds,
sea ducks came from the deep,
and swans from the watery fens.
Even little larks and finches,
chirping carolers by the hundreds,
came chattering on buoyant wings
to revel in the sound.

The very spirits of nature,
lovely daughters of the air,
glowing on the rainbow
or gleaming on a pink-fringed cloud
wondered at the joyance.

There was no fish of the deep
that did not come to listen:
the pike came wallowing along,
salmon and whitefish from bottoms and reefs,
even the little perch and roach
swam up close to the shore
to listen to Väinö's song.

Old Ahto, lord of the waters,
sedge-bearded king of the waves,
vowed he had never heard the like.
The sedgy-breasted water lady
came paddling through the waves
to rest on a bed of reeds
and listen to the sound.

41: 13-161

## Selfishness

A grouse is too scanty for two,
so is a squirrel split in three.
It's best I keep watch on the Sampo,
control the great mill myself.

42: 45-52

## Do something!

Weeping won't do at sea,
bawling's no good in a boat!
Tears won't dispel a danger,
nor wailing avert evil days.

42: 523-526

# Music

Every last man stood around
hands gripping a cloth cap,
every woman who heard
stood with hands clasped to her breast...
Every beast of the woods
settled down on its paws
to hear the kantele play
to take in the joy of the sound.
Birds that fly through the air
perched themselves on a limb,
Fish of all sorts in the flood
hurried up to the shore.
Even the worms underground
squirmed to the surface to listen,
wriggled up to hear the sweet sound,
the kantele's lasting delight...

44: 273-305

*Mi oli miehiä lähellä,*
*ne kaikki lakit käessä;*
*mi oli akkoja lähellä,*
*ne kaikki käsi posella.*
*Mi oli metsän eläintä,*
*kyykistyivät kynsillehen*
*kanteloista kuulemahan,*
*iloa imehtimähän.*
*Ilman linnut lentäväiset*

*varvuille varustelihe,*
*veen kalaset kaikenlaiset*
*rantahan rakentelihe.*
*Matosetki maanalaiset*
*päälle mullan muuttelihe*
*—käänteleivät, kuuntelevat*
*tuota soittoa suloista,*
*kantelen iki-iloa...*

44: 273-305

## Guests

If a visitor is welcome,
fling the doors wide open for him.
If it's someone you detest,
slam them shut with all your strength.

46: 183-186

# Yearning

I wished as one does for a good year,
watched as for the coming of summer,
waited like a ski for new snow
to make the gliding easy,
like a maid for her lover to come,
a red-cheeked girl for her mate.

46: 201-206

## Gloomy Finns?

Let the days be filled with music,
and the nights with merrymaking,
all across this clime and country,
on the spacious farms of Finland,
among the young folk of the future,
the rising generation.

46: 639-644

# Fisherman's prayer

Ahto, master of the waves,
ruler of a hundred sea caves!
Take a rod five fathoms long,
or take one, say, of seven,
with it scour the main,
stir up the ocean depths,
drive all the finny flock,
stir up the fishy herd,
straight to our fishing place,
the spot where we drop our nets.
Drive the fish from the chasms,
the salmon from the caves,
up from the poles of the sea,
up from the gloomy depths,
where the sun never shines,
where the sand never shifts!

48: 135-150

## Charm for burns

Fetch frost from the North,
ice from the region of chill!
The North has frost aplenty,
it is the frozen zone.
Frozen are the streams,
the air is all glare ice;
frozen rabbits caper,
frozen bears cavort,
among the hills of snow,
on slopes of snow mountains,
frozen swans row slowly along,
frozen ducklings paddle,
out in a river of snow,
on the rim of the icy wilds.
Bring cold in on your sled,
haul ice in on your runners…

48: 333-346

# Substitutes

Oh Ilmarinen, you silly smith!
Now that is a stupid plan!
Gold will never glow like moonlight.
Silver never shine like sunlight.

49: 55-58

# Childbirth prayer

Come Creator merciful,   free a maid from torment,
my shelter and my God,   from the strain of birth,
in this time of trial,   lest she be overcome
in these painful pangs,   and sink into the shadows.

50: 307-314

## Väinämöinen's prophecy

Let time go by,
and day succeed to day;
the day will come
when I'll be called for, needed,
to fetch another Sampo,
restore the kantele,
bring back the moon,
set free the sun,
when both the sun and moon are lost,
and there is no joy on earth.

50: 491-500

## Väinämöinen's legacy

There he ceased his sailing,
rested from his weary journey.
Left the kantele behind him,
Finland's tuneful instrument,
left his great songs to his children,
a lasting legacy of joy.

50: 507-512

# Lönnrot's *valedictory*

Time for me to cease my singing,
tie my tongue up in a knot....
I'll wind my verse up in a ball...
stow it in the storehouse loft....
Many have complained to me,
cursed my verse or damned my accent...

But still in all, at any rate,
I have broken trail for others,
set the course and cleared the way
for better, more prolific singers,
for the younger folk,
for the rising generation.

50: 611-620

# Selective Glossary

**Aino:** younger sister of Joukahainen, promised in marriage to old Väinämöinen.

**Hiisi:** the spirit of mischief, chief among demons.

**Ilmatar:** spirit of the air, (ilma-air) Väinämöinen's mother and creator of the earth.

**Ilmarinen:** mighty smith who forged the Sampo and the dome of the sky.

**Joukahainen:** a young Lapp, brother Aino, who foolishly challenges Väinämöinen to a singing duel.

**Jumala:** God, but meaning varies in *Kalevala* from "spirit" to the Christian Deity.

**Kaleva:** (Osmo) mythical ancestor of many characters in the epic.

**kantele:** Finland's "national" instrument, a kind of harp, originally five-stringed (Väinämöinen's kantele).

**Kalervo:** father of Kullervo, whose feud with his brother Untamo leads to the tragedy of Kullervo.

**Kullervo:** a tragic hero, son of Kalervo, who commits incest with his sister.

**Kyllikki:** the greatest beauty among the island girls and the (at first) reluctant wife of Lemminkäinen.

**Lemminkäinen:** (aka. Kaukomieli, Ahti) "lover-boy;" tag word "lieto" (light, wayward) is constantly applied to him.

**Louhi:** the mistress of Pohjola, whose character varies from hospitable hostess to wicked witch.

**Marjatta:** virgin mother whose child supplants Väinämöinen at the close of the epic.

**Sampsa Pellervoinen:** an earth spirit who sows the first crops.

**Master of Pohjola:** see Pohjola below.

**Otava:** Ursa Major, the Great Bear (Big Dipper) constellation associated with the birth of the bear and the ritual of the bear hunt.

**Pohjola:** the North or North Farm; meanings range from a prosperous farm to a tribal area to a cold, man-devouring place.

**Sampo:** the magic mill forged by Ilmarinen, whose reward is marriage to the daughter of Pohjola.

**Tiera:** Lemminkäinen's companion on an abortive raid on Pohjola (literally a chunk of packed snow on a boot or horse's hoof).

**Tuonela:** land of the dead.

**Ukko:** the chief God; cf. Jumala, above.

**Untamo:** spirit of sleep; also the name of Kalervo's brother.

**Väinämöinen:** greatest of wise men and singers, inventor of the kantele; tag phrase "old, steady" usually accompanies his name.

**Antero Vipunen:** a sleeping giant to whom Väinämöinen goes in search of knowledge.

**Virokannas:** a Karelian braggart. Also, in the Marjatta episode, a man called in to judge the case of the child.

**Wet-hat:** a blind herdsman, dismissed by Lemminkäinen as beneath contempt, causes his death.

# A Guide to Reading the *Kalevala*

This guide, to accompany the reading of the *Kalevala*, is based on Elias Lönnrot's introductory notes to each runo.

**Runo 1.** *Prelude.* Lönnrot as poet tells of his yearning to sing the poems of his people, joining hands with a fellow singer. The close link between poetry and nature is aptly described in lines that speak of the frost singing verses, the rain reciting them, etc.

    *Creation of the world and the birth of* **Väinämöinen.** Ilmatar, the virgin of the air, leaves the loneliness of the skies and goes to the sea, where she is made pregnant by the wind. She drifts for ages on the water, unable to give birth. A scaup duck comes flying by looking for a place to rest. Ilmatar raises a knee as a place for her to light on. The bird lands, lays her eggs, and broods on them. The heat of her brooding causes Ilmatar to jerk her knee back into the water. One of the eggs is transformed: the lower half becomes the earth, the upper half becomes the sky, the yolk becomes the sun, and the white becomes the moon. In her wanderings, Ilmatar shapes the landscapes of the earth and sea. Still unborn after thirty years in his mother's womb, Väinämöinen forces his way out. He has to float at sea for another eight years before he reaches land.

**Runo 2.** *Origin of plants.* After years on land, Väinämöinen gets **Sampsa Pellervoinen** to plant trees. All varieties thrive, except for the oak, for which another seed is obtained. Tursas, a gnome from the sea, burns hay which has been sown by five water nymphs. An acorn is sown in the ashes. The oak which grows from it is so huge that it blots out the sun, and there is no one able to cut it down.

Finally a tiny man emerges from the sea. He is suddenly transformed into a giant and fells the oak with three blows of his ax. The sun shines again; there are trees, grass, and berries, but no barley as yet. A titmouse tells Väinämöinen that no barley will grow until he cuts down the trees. Väinämöinen does so, leaving only one birch tree standing. An eagle comes by and is so pleased that Väinämöinen has left the tree as a perch for him, that he strikes fire to burn the trees felled for the planting. Väinämöinen plants his barley and it begins to grow. The runo ends with the happy spring-time song of the cuckoo.

**Runo 3.** *The singing duel.* Väinämöinen grows in fame and knowledge. **Joukahainen,** a Lapp, hears about him and challenges him to a singing duel. Angry at being worsted, Joukahainen draws his sword, but Väinämöinen sings him neck-deep into a swamp. Joukahainen promises Väinämöinen a number of things in exchange for being freed, but Väinämöinen relents only when Joukahainen promises his sister Aino to Väinämöinen as a bride. **Aino** is stricken at the news, but her mother is pleased at the prospect of her daughter's marrying a powerful man.

**Runo 4.** *The death of Aino.* Väinämöinen sees Aino gathering sauna *vihtas* and tells her to dress and primp herself only for him. Aino tears off her jewels and goes home weeping. Her mother tries to console her but Aino cannot stand the thought of being an old man's bride. She goes to bathe in the sea, and the rock on which she is sitting suddenly plunges into the water. Her mother weeps the death of her daughter and moralizes: "Never try to trick your daughter... / To accept your choice of husband…"

**Runo 5.** *Aino lost again.* Grieving for the loss of Aino, Väinämöinen asks **Untamo,** the spirit of sleep, where the sea maidens dwell. He goes to fish for them, catches a steelhead, which he is about to clean when it slips back into the water. It is Aino, who taunts him for having lost her a second time. He goes home heavy-hearted. His mother Ilmatar advises him to go and court one of the daughters of the North (**Pohjola**).

**Runo 6.** *Joukahainen's revenge.* Joukahainen sees Väinämöinen crossing a river on horseback on his way to Pohjola. He shoots arrows at him, but only manages to kill his horse. Väinämöinen is driven far out to sea and drifts at the mercy of the waves. Joukahainen goes home exultant.

**Runo 7.** *Väinämöinen's rescue and vow.* After drifting for days, Väinämöinen is rescued by the eagle, who is thankful for his having left the tree for birds to perch on. The bird leaves him in Pohjola, where a maid doing the laundry on the shore hears him weeping. **Louhi, the mistress of Pohjola,** takes him in and entertains him well, but Väinämöinen is anxious to return home. Louhi promises him a horse for the return journey, and also promises her daughter in marriage to the man who can forge the **Sampo.** Väinämöinen says he will get the smith **Ilmarinen** to forge the great mill. Louhi gives him the horse and warns him not to look up on his return journey.

**Runo 8.** *Väinämöinen's wound.* Väinämöinen looks up and sees the lovely maid of Pohjola sitting on a rainbow weaving. He tries to persuade her to come into his sleigh, but she refuses. They debate the merits of single and married life. She proposes a number of tasks for him: to tie an egg into a knot, split a horsehair with a dull knife, peel birch bark from a stone. The last task is to build a boat from the splinters of her spindle, etc. On the third day that he is working on the boat, Väinämöinen's ax rebounds from a rock and cuts a gash in his leg from knee to toe. He tries to stem the flow of blood, but has forgotten a part of the blood-stopping charm and drives off in his sleigh to find someone who knows it. He finally finds an old man who says that he has stopped worse bleeding.

**Runo 9.** *The cure.* The old man has forgotten the birth of iron, which is a part of the cure. Väinämöinen recites it and the old man says the rest of the charm, stopping the flow of blood. He sends his son to fetch ointments and salves, and binds the wound. Väinämöinen is healed. He warns people against taking up boat-building on a dare, and to acquiesce in the will of **Jumala.**

**Runo 10.** *Forging the Sampo.* Väinämöinen returns home and urges Ilmarinen to go to Pohjola and forge the Sampo. Ilmarinen refuses and Väinämöinen tricks him by singing a beautiful tree with the Great Bear (**Ursa Major**) on its branches and the moon on its crown. Ilmarinen climbs after the moon and a whirlwind catches him up and carries him to Pohjola. He is well received and sets to work forging the Sampo. On one side it is a flour mill, on another, a salt mill, and on the third, a money mill. When it is finished, the mistress of Pohjola locks it up in the Rock Mountain. Ilmarinen asks for the girl's hand, but she says, "Sorry, I'm too busy now." Dejected, he goes home and tells Väinämöinen that the Sampo is forged and is busy grinding grain for Pohjola.

**Runo 11.** *The exploits of Lemminkäinen* (**aka. Kaukomieli, Ahti**). Lemminkäinen is a handsome scamp and a playboy. **Kyllikki** is an island maiden, beautiful, sought-after, but unattainable. He goes to the island to woo her, and sleeps with most of the women there in the process. She continues to refuse him, and finally he carries her off by force. He promises to treat her well, and at last she yields, making him promise that he will never go to war. He in turn asks her to promise that she will not go to dances or revels with the village girls. She agrees, and they return to Lemminkäinen's home. His mother is delighted with her daughter-in-law.

**Runo 12.** *The broken promise.* Lemminkäinen goes off to gather fish roe. While he is gone, Kyllikki goes to dance with the girls in the village. Lemminkäinen's sister **Ainikki** tells him about it, and he angrily gets ready to go off to war. His mother begs him not to go, saying that he will be killed. He throws down his hair brush, saying that he will not die until the hair brush bleeds. He arrives in Pohjola, defeats and scatters all the Pohjola wizards in a singing contest, leaving only **Wet-hat,** an ugly herdsman, whom he considers beneath contempt. Wet-hat runs to the River of Tuonela to lie in wait and revenge himself on Lemminkäinen.

**Runo 13.** *Skiing the elk of* **Hiisi.** Lemminkäinen asks Louhi for one of her daughters. She refuses, saying that he can ask only after he has skied down the elk of Hiisi. He goes to Kauppi, the ski-maker, for a pair of skis. The demons hear him boasting about capturing the elk, and make an animal of wood for him to chase. Lemminkäinen does catch it, but it bolts and he starts after it, breaking his skis.

**Runo 14.** *The death of Lemminkäinen.* With the aid of forest spirits summoned by hunters' charms, Lemminkäinen succeeds in capturing the elk. The mistress of Pohjola sets him the further tasks of bridling the horse of Hiisi and shooting the swan of Tuonela. He accomplishes the first, but on his way to shoot the swan, he is pierced by a poisoned arrow from the bow of Wet-hat. Not knowing the charm for the poison, he dies and is thrown into the river. The son of Tuoni chops him to pieces.

**Runo 15.** *Lemminkäinen's resurrection.* Waiting for Lemminkäinen's return, his mother and Kyllikki, his wife, see blood running from the hair brush. His mother rushes off to Pohjola to find her son. At first the mistress of Pohjola denies knowing where he is, but finally admits that he has gone to shoot the swan of Tuonela. The sun tells Lemminkäinen's mother what has happened to Lemminkäinen, and she goes to Ilmarinen to have him forge a rake. With it she retrieves her son's dismembered body from below the rapids in the River of Tuonela and pieces it together with the aid of appropriate charms. To restore life to the body, she sends the bee to get an ointment from the Creator's storehouse. Lemminkäinen returns home with his mother, and the singer goes on to other stories.

**Runo 16.** *The voyage to Tuonela.* Väinämöinen sends Sampsa Pellervoinen to get wood for a boat he is building. Sampsa passes up an aspen, which tells him it is rotten inside, and a pine, which tells him a raven has thrice croaked in its branches. He takes an oak, which tells him it is good for building a boat. Väinämöinen begins to sing the boat, but he has forgotten a part of the charm and decides to go to the nether world of **Tuonela** to get it. To get there, Väinämöinen pretends to have died a natural death, but only when he tells the truth is Tuoni's daughter willing to ferry him across the River of Tuonela. Once he is there, the old man of Tuonela tries to keep him there by weaving a net across the river, but Väinämöinen changes himself into an otter and slips through the net. Having returned, he warns the people not to go to Tuonela and tells them of the awful state of the guilty there.

**Runo 17.** *In the belly of the giant.* Having failed to get the boat-building charm from Tuonela, Väinämöinen, prompted by a herdsman, decides to seek it from **Antero Vipunen.** He is told that to reach the giant, he will have to walk first over the points of women's needles, next over the tips of swords, and then over the blades of battle axes. To do so, he has Ilmarinen forge protective armor for him. He finds the giant sleeping, with trees growing from his body. He cuts down the trees and pries open the mouth of the giant, who awakens. Väinämöinen slips and falls into the mouth and is swallowed by the giant. In the giant's belly, Väinämöinen first makes a boat and rows through all the abdominal passageways. Then he sets up a forge, which so torments Vipunen that the giant sings all the charms he knows. Väinämöinen leaps out of his mouth, returns home, and completes the boat.

**Runo 18.** *The rival suitors.* Väinämöinen sets sail for Pohjola to court the daughter of the North. Ilmarinen's sister Annikki sees his boat pass by and tells her brother that Väinämöinen is setting off to get the girl who has been promised to Ilmarinen, who in turn sets off by sleigh. Seeing them coming, the mistress of Pohjola advises her daughter to choose Väinämöinen, but the girl says she will go to the forger of the

Sampo, and tells Väinämöinen, who arrives first, that she does not care for him.

**Runo 19.** *Ilmarinen's tasks and betrothal.* Ilmarinen arrives at the house of Pohjola, asks for the hand of the girl, and is assigned a number of tasks he must perform in order to win her. With the help of the girl, he is able to plow a field of snakes, shackle the bear of Tuoni, and muzzle the wolf of Tuoni. To capture a huge pike from the river of Tuoni, the last of his chores, Ilmarinen forges a gigantic eagle, which captures the fish. Then he claims his bride. A child speaks up from the floor and compares his coming to Pohjola to the arrival of a hawk that carries off the sweetest of chicks from a flock. But the child concludes by saying that it is impossible to keep young girls hidden from men. Väinämöinen goes home crestfallen, advising old men never to try competing in courtship with younger men.

**Runo 20.** *Wedding preparations — killing the ox and brewing the ale.* There is a huge ox in Karelia, but no one can be found to slaughter it. Virokannas, the Karelian, boasts that he will kill it, but when the animal tosses its head, he scurries up a tree. A little man emerges from the sea and kills the gigantic beast. An old man from atop the oven recites the origins of ale, and ale is brewed and food prepared for the wedding. Messengers are sent to invite everyone to the feast; Lemminkäinen alone is not invited.

**Runo 21.** *The wedding feast.* The groom's party is welcomed with elaborate ceremony and hospitality. They are feasted and the question of who will be the singer comes up. A child on the floor offers to sing, but is rebuffed. An old man tells what a great singer he had been before he lost his voice. Finally Väinämöinen sings, to the great joy of everyone. But he reminds them that if Jumala were to sing, he would "sing the seas to honey and the sand to peas."

**Runo 22.** *Single and wedded "bliss."* The bride is prepared for her departure and is given dire warnings about what she may find as a daughter-in-law in her new home. She is told to weep for what she is leaving and for what may lie ahead. The bride weeps, saying that she had not thought of these things before, but a child from the floor consoles her by saying that she is going to a better place and is getting a good man.

**Runo 23.** *The instruction of the bride.* The bride is advised to be diligent and hard-working, to obey her husband and to honor her new family, even though they may be harsh and cruel. An old woman on the floor who is now a wandering beggar tells the story of her marriage to a brute and of her life with his family, which she left when she could stand it no longer.

**Runo 24.** *The instruction of the groom.* The groom is told what a fine bride he has and is advised to treat her kindly. If she does not obey, she is to be taught first with words, then with looks, then with a reed switch, then with a slender wood switch, etc. An old man on the floor tells how he tamed an unruly wife with a rod. The bride says goodbye to her parents, weeping at the thought that they may be gone when she returns. The couple leaves as the children sing a song about how much they will miss her. Ilmarinen and his bride arrive at his home in three days.

**Runo 25.** *The welcome home.* The bridal party has been eagerly awaited. It is welcomed by the mother-in-law, who tells the bride that she has come to a good home. A child mocks Ilmarinen from the floor, saying he has brought an ugly bride, but she is scolded and the bride is praised. All are feasted, and Väinämöinen sings, praising all the members of the household. On his way home Väinämöinen wrecks his sleigh and has to make a journey to Tuonela for an auger to repair it. That accomplished, he completes the journey home.

**Runo 26.** *Lemminkäinen goes to Pohjola.* Angry at not having been invited to the wedding, Lemminkäinen decides to go to Pohjola anyway. His mother warns him against going, telling him that his way will be blocked first by a flaming river where an eagle sits on an island, ready to tear apart all strangers, then by a blazing trench filled with hot stones, then by a wolf and a bear, and finally by a fence of lances interwoven with snakes and lizards, which reaches from earth to heaven. On the ground are more hissing adders, one a serpent larger than all the rest. Still intent on going, Lemminkäinen boasts of all the dangers he has escaped in the past. His mother warns him against wizards who will enchant and kill him. She describes a hillside covered with stakes capped with human heads, with one remaining uncapped for his own head. But, overcoming all the obstacles, Lemminkäinen goes to Pohjola.

**Runo 27.** *The confrontation at Pohjola.* Lemminkäinen barges into the house at Pohjola and demands food and drink. He is offered a rancid stew with worms in it, and insults the **master of Pohjola** by offering to pay for some ale. The latter conjures up a pond on the floor and tells him to drink from it. The two engage in a conjuring competition, and the master of Pohjola, unable to defeat Lemminkäinen, draws his sword. Lemminkäinen gives him the two first blows, which he misses, then slices off his head and sets it on the one empty stake. The mistress of Pohjola conjures up a whole army of swordsmen and Lemminkäinen is forced to flee.

**Runo 28.** *Lemminkäinen's flight.* Lemminkäinen returns home to his mother and begs her to tell him where he can hide from the men of Pohjola. She scolds him for having gone there, reviews possible hiding places, and then tells him to go to a faraway island where his father had once taken refuge during a war.

**Runo 29.** *Lemminkäinen on the island of women.* Lemminkäinen sails to the island of women, where "...he knew a thousand brides, / Slept beside a hundred widows." The men of the island plan to kill him, but he escapes in time. Both he and the women lament his departure. A storm wrecks his ship, but he swims to land, gets a new ship, and returns home. He finds the house burned down and the place abandoned, but his mother is still alive and hiding in the forest. She tells him of their home's destruction by the forces of Pohjola. He promises her a new and better home, and tells her of his happy life on the island, where, he says, he shunned the women "the way a hawk does the village chickens."

**Runo 30.** *Ice-bound.* Lemminkäinen hears a warship weeping because it is lying idle, and decides to make war on Pohjola. He gets a friend, **Tiera,** to accompany him and the two set sail. The wife of Pohjola sends the frost to freeze him, and the ship is stuck fast in the ice. Lemminkäinen overcomes frost with a charm and the men walk across the ice to the shore, where he conjures up a horse and the two ride home. The poet states that he will shift to another story.

**Runo 31.** *The misfit Kullervo.* Two Karelian brothers, **Untamo** and **Kalervo,** are feuding with each other. Untamo finally attacks Kalervo's home and destroys it, carrying off the only apparent survivor, a pregnant woman. A son, **Kullervo,** is born to her. On the third day after his birth, he kicks the cradle to pieces, and at the age of three months he vows to take revenge on Untamo for his family's death. Untamo tries to drown, burn, and hang the child, but the boy survives all the attempts. Untamo gives up and tries to put him to work as a slave. Kullervo, assigned to care for a child, lets it die; set to clearing the woods, he destroys the finest timber; ordered to work on fences, he builds one with no gate that stretches from earth to sky. In disgust, Untamo sells him to Ilmarinen as a slave.

**Runo 32.** *The charm for letting cattle out to pasture.* The wife of Ilmarinen sends Kullervo out to tend the cattle. She gives him a loaf of bread for his lunch but bakes a large stone in its center as a cruel practical joke. She recites a long charm that is used when the cattle are sent out to pasture.

**Runo 33.** *Milking the wild beasts.* In the afternoon, Kullervo tries to slice the bread for his lunch, but breaks his knife on the stone hidden in it. Angry at the destruction of this last memento of his father, he meditates revenge. A crow in a thicket suggests that he drive the cattle into a bog and drive home a transformed herd of wolves and bears in their place. Kullervo does so, and arrives tooting a horn made of cattle bones. When Ilmarinen's wife (praised in other runos as a great beauty — now described as the "sneer-mouthed wife of Ilmarinen") starts milking one of the animals, they begin tearing her to pieces. She begs Kullervo to reverse the charm, but he refuses.

**Runo 34.** *Family reunion.* Kullervo goes off tooting his cow horn. Ilmari hears the sound, discovers his dead wife, and mourns her. Kullervo sits lamenting his fate and decides to take revenge on Untamo for the death of his parents. An old woman of the woods tells him that his family is still alive. He in united with them and hears their story. One of his sisters has been lost while picking berries.

**Runo 35.** *Kullervo's tragic deed.* Kullervo's father tries his son at various jobs, but with his misguided muscle, Kullervo makes a mess of everything he does. He is sent off to pay the taxes (in grain). On the way back, he meets his lost sister. Not knowing who she is, he inveigles her into his sleigh and commits incest with her. When she discovers his identity, she leaps off the sleigh and throws herself into a rapids. Kullervo rushes home and tells his family what he has done. He contemplates suicide, but his mother pleads with him not to end his life. He decides to go and take revenge on Untamo.

**Runo 36.** *The death of Kullervo.* Kullervo prepares himself for battle and says goodbye to his family. When he asks them in turn if they care whether he lives or dies, only his mother answers yes. On his way to Untamola (the home of Untamo), messages arrive telling him of the deaths of his father, brother, and sister. For each of them, he has only one comment: "If he's dead — so what, he's dead." Only the news of his mother's death moves him, but he does not turn back. He destroys

Untamola, setting the buildings on fire. When he returns home, he finds the place deserted except for a black dog, with which he goes to hunt for food. When he comes across the place where he had seduced his sister (no grass or flowers grow on the spot), he commits suicide by falling on his sword.

**Runo 37.** *The gold-and-silver bride.* Grieving for his wife, Ilmarinen forges a woman from gold and silver. But he cannot bring her to life, and when he sleeps with her, he wakes up with the side that has been next to her freezing cold. He tries to palm her off on Väinämöinen, who tells him either to melt her down and make tools of her, or send her off to Germany or Russia. The runo ends with Väinämöinen urging people never to bow down to gold or silver, or young men to court gold-and-silver women.

**Runo 38.** *Ilmarinen's second courtship.* Ilmari goes to Pohjola to court another daughter of the North. Louhi laments having given him her first daughter, reviles him, and vows that she will not repeat the error. He asks the daughter herself to go, and when she refuses, he carries her off by force. On the way back she treats him to a tongue-lashing and spends the first night on the road laughing with another man. In disgust, he transforms her into a sea gull. He meets Väinämöinen and tells him what he has done with the girl, and that the people of Pohjola are prospering with the Sampo.

**Runo 39.** *The raid on Pohjola.* Väinämöinen urges Ilmarinen to go with him to Pohjola to bring back the Sampo. He wants to go by sea, but Ilmarinen prefers to go by land. Ilmarinen forges a sword for Väinämöinen and the two don their armor. They hitch up the horse, but on their way along the shore they hear the sound of weeping. It is a warship weeping because it lies rotting away with worms eating it and nasty birds nesting in it. Väinämöinen sings the ship onto the sea, then sings the benches on one side full of men and those on the other side full of women. But no one can row the boat until Ilmarinen takes the oars. On the way they pass Lemminkäinen, who asks to go along. They take him on board gladly; he brings extra planking with him to raise the sides of the ship.

**Runo 40.** *The pike-bone kantele.* The ship comes to a rapids and is grounded below it on the back of a huge pike. Väinämöinen tells Lemminkäinen to cut the pike in half with his sword, but Lemminkäinen falls into the water when he tries to and has to be pulled out. Väinämöinen kills the pike, half of which falls back into the water. They land on an island, cook the fish and eat it, leaving only the bones. Looking at them, Väinämöinen decides that he can make a kantele from the jawbone. He makes tuning pegs from the pike's teeth and strings it with horsehair from the gelding of Hiisi. All the others try to play it, but none succeed.

**Runo 41.** *Väinämöinen plays the kantele.* As Väinämöinen plays the new instrument, all things — land animals, fish from the sea, birds of the air, even the spirits of nature — flock to listen. They are so moved by the music that they all weep. The tears of Väinämöinen roll into the sea. A duck goes to fetch them and they are found to have changed into pearls.

**Runo 42.** *Capture of the Sampo.* The men of Kaleva arrive in Pohjola. Väinämöinen asks Louhi if she will share the Sampo with him. She refuses and he tells her they will take it by force. Angered, she summons all the young men with their swords. Väinämöinen puts them all to sleep by playing the kantele, and the three men go to the copper mountain, where the Sampo is kept behind nine locks. Väinämöinen is able to open the locks by chanting, but they cannot lift the Sampo, the roots of which go down nine fathoms. Lemminkäinen plows up the roots with the great ox of Pohjola and they leave with the Sampo on board ship. On the third day Lemminkäinen decides that they should have some music and starts to sing. His bellowing startles a crane, which flies off squawking and awakens the wife of Pohjola. She sends a fog to slow up the vessel, calls on the sea monster Turso to kill the men of Kaleva, and raises a furious storm. The kantele is blown overboard and lost. Lemminkäinen adds planking to the sides of the ship and they ride out the storm.

**Runo 43.** *The sea battle for the Sampo.* Louhi, the wife of Pohjola, musters an army and sets sail in pursuit of the Sampo. Väinämöinen, seeing that they cannot outrun her ship, conjures up a reef that wrecks it. Louhi turns herself into a huge eagle, takes hundreds of bow- and swordsmen under her wings and onto her tail, and alights on the mast of the ship. Väinämöinen smashes her claws with the rudder, and her men fall into the sea, but she is able to knock the Sampo overboard as she falls. Väinämöinen sees the pieces of the Sampo drifting shoreward and interprets the fact as a good omen. Louhi threatens to lock up the sun and the moon and send diseases to Kaleva. Väinämöinen goes ashore, collects and sows the pieces of the Sampo, and prays to Jumala to pro-tect the people of Kaleva.

**Runo 44.** *The new kantele.* Feeling the need for music again, Väinämöinen asks Ilmarinen to forge a rake to search for the pike-bone kantele. Unable to find it, he makes a completely new instrument from birch, with pegs of oak and strings from a maiden's hair. Again all living beings respond to his playing.

**Runo 45.** *The plague.* Hearing of the happiness in Kaleva, Louhi sends diseases to afflict the people there. A long passages describes the origin of illnesses. Väinämöinen heats the sauna, and with powerful charms and ointments, he sends the aches and pains to Pain Mountain and cures the people.

**Runo 46.** *The ceremony of the bear hunt.* Hearing that the people of Kaleva have escaped the plague, Louhi, the gap-toothed wife of Pohjola, sends a bear to wreak havoc on their cattle. Väinämöinen kills the bear and they hold the customary feast. The bear is treated as an object of respect — he has not been slain, but has tumbled from the tree himself. The feast is in his honor, and he is greeted as a long-awaited and welcome guest. Väinämöinen sings the birth of the bear, who "was not born on straw...[but] ...yonder by the Moon... / On the shoulders of the Great Bear..." Väinämöinen plays and sings, to the delight of the audience, and concludes with a prayer for the welfare of Kaleva.

**Runo 47.** *Theft of the sun and the moon.* The sun and the moon come and perch on tree limbs to listen to Väinämöinen playing the kantele. Louhi steals them, hides the sun in a steel mountain and the moon in a rock cave. She even steals fire from the people of Kaleva, leaving them in darkness. **Ukko, the chief god,** wonders at the darkness and strikes a spark, from which he plans to create a new sun and moon.

The maid who is set to nurse the spark lets it slip through her fingers and it falls to earth. Väinämöinen and Ilmarinen set out to find it. Ilmatar tells them that the fire, after causing great damage, has fallen into Lake Alue, causing the lake to boil over its banks. The fire is swallowed first by a whitefish, which in turn is swallowed by a sea trout, which is then swallowed by a pike. Väinämöinen and Ilmarinen weave a fiber net with which to catch the pike, but do not succeed.

**Runo 48.** *The quest for fire.* Väinämöinen has a huge net woven of linen, and with it they succeed in catching the pike with the other fish and the fire in its belly. As the son of Day is cleaning the fish, the fire again escapes. It singes Väinämöinen's beard, scorches Ilmarinen's face, and burns down half the forests in the country. Väinämöinen captures the fire and returns it to its proper place in the homes of Kaleva. Ilmarinen cures his burns with the aid of a frost charm.

**Runo 49.** *Freeing the sun and moon.* Ilmarinen forges a new sun and moon, but they give no light. Väinämöinen casts lots and learns where the sun and moon are hidden. He goes to Pohjola, defeats the men there, but cannot open the locks and bars imprisoning the sun and moon. He returns to have Ilmarinen forge tools with which to open the locks. While Ilmarinen is working at his forge, Louhi comes in the shape of a hawk to ask what he is making. He tells her he is forging an iron collar to chain the wife of Pohjola to the side of a strong mountain. Feeling that she is doomed, Louhi releases the sun and the moon. Changing herself to a dove, she flies back to Ilmarinen to tell him that the sun and the moon are once more in the sky.

**Runo 50.** *The story of* **Marjatta** *and the farewell of* *Väinämöinen.* The virgin Marjatta lives for a long time in the house of her father. So chaste is she that she will have nothing to do with an animal if it has been so much as bred. One day while herding the sheep, she swallows a lingonberry, which makes her pregnant. When her time comes to give birth, she asks her mother and father to warm the sauna, but they drive her off as a whore. Finally she goes to a stable, where the breath of a mare serves as the sauna steam, and gives birth to a son. She keeps him in seclusion, but one day he disappears. Searching for him she asks a star, the moon, and the sun if they know where he is. The sun tells her he is in a swamp, where she finds him. They look for someone to christen the boy and old **Virokannas** comes to do it, but insists that the child first be questioned to find out if he should be permitted to live. Väinämöinen is called to pronounce judgment on the child. He decides that since the boy is descended from a berry of the earth, he should be planted in the earth. But the boy accuses him of false judgment and of causing the death of Aino. He also accuses him of Joukahainen's crime — offering his sister to save his own life. Angry and ashamed, Väinämöinen sings himself a boat and sails off in it, saying that a time will come when the people will need him again. But he leaves his kantele and his songs to the country.

# Lönnrot's Epilogue

"Now I will end my song. People
may find fault with my verses, but
I have broken track, shown the
way for better singers."

*The words are Lönnrot's closing comments on his role as a
poet and a contributor to the tradition of Finnish poetry.*